This book belongs to:

Jamie Lee Carey

Happy 3ʳᵈ Birthday 7-19-99
With love from Meemom & Boppop

Favorite Bible Heroes

Favorite Bible Heroes

Tommy NELSON™

Thomas Nelson, Inc.
Nashville

Featuring these
Children's Bible Classics:

1. **Noah and the Ark**

2. **Joseph and the Coat of Many Colors**

3. **The Story of Moses**

In the years after the time of Adam and Eve and their children, the world had become a very bad place where people disobeyed God's laws and did evil things.

In this bad world, there lived a very good man named Noah. He and his family lived a peaceful, quiet life. They obeyed God's laws and loved each other.

God was angry with the people who did not listen to Him. He decided to start over by washing the world clean with a huge Flood. God spoke to Noah and told him that he should save himself and his family by building a large boat, called an Ark.

When Noah and his family began to work on the Ark, their neighbors asked them why they were building a huge boat so far from the sea. Noah told them what God had said, but they laughed at him and called him crazy. He tried to get them to change their ways.

At last, the Ark was finished. God told Noah to load the Ark with enough food for his family and for the animals that would be coming. The first animals to get on the Ark may have been the pet cats and dogs that lived with Noah's family.

The news of the coming Flood spread to the creatures in the nearby woods . . . to the squirrels, the bunnies, the birds, and even old Mr. and Mrs. Mole.

The news was heard by the bears and the deer, the squirrels and the owls in the deep forests. They had to hurry to Noah's Ark.

From the cool, green woods, the news traveled over the rocky deserts. The camels, the buzzards and lizards and even the jackals knew that something important was about to happen.

The news was heard high in the mountains. The goats, the llamas, and the eagles knew they must come to join the other animals on the Ark.

God's message found its way into the thick jungles. The giraffes and the hippos, the tigers and the zebras knew they must hurry to the Ark. The monkeys laughed at the news but they quickly followed the other animals.

The Ark was an amazing sight. Hundreds of animals were streaming to the Ark, two by two. There were lions and tigers and polar bears. There were cows and zebras. There were turtles and turkeys. There were snakes and dragonflies.

Animals were coming from the ends of the Earth. There were bunnies, squirrels, bears, elephants, and kangaroos.

As the last of the animals scampered aboard, Noah noticed the first raindrops of the storm that God had said would bring the great Flood. Soon it would be raining harder than it had ever rained before. Noah and his family entered the Ark and God closed the door.

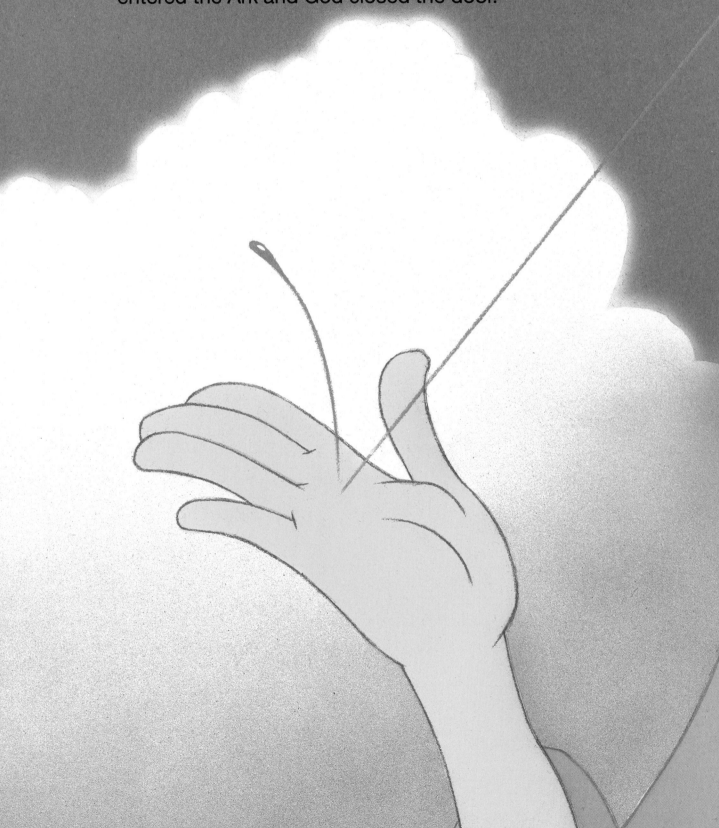

Suddenly, there was a loud clap of thunder and the rain began to come down very hard. Inside the Ark, everyone was cozy and dry. Even the lions were peaceful for a change, and even the little lambs were not afraid of them.

The wind blew and the rain poured. The Flood came, the waters rose, and soon the Ark was floating free.

It rained for forty days and forty nights. At last, God decided that the Earth had been washed clean. Noah turned to his wife and said, "I think the rain has stopped! Maybe we can land soon."

After many days had passed, Noah decided to send a raven out the window to see if there was a dry place for the bird to land.

The raven just flew around and around, and couldn't find a place to land. The next day Noah sent a dove out to see what she could find. She came back with a green olive branch in her beak. That meant the water had gone down, and somewhere plants were starting to grow again. Noah and his family were overjoyed.

A week later, Noah let the dove go again. This time, the dove didn't return. This meant that the water had gone down and she had found a place to build her nest. The great Flood was over.

Noah and his family praised God and thanked him for keeping them safe. Time passed and the world would soon be filled with people and animals again. Only this time, it was a lot more peaceful.

God promised that He would never again flood the whole Earth. To remind everyone of that promise, He made the first rainbow, and put it in the sky. Even now, when we see a rainbow after a storm, we remember God's promise—and Noah, and the Ark.

JOSEPH AND THE
COAT OF MANY COLORS

A long time ago, in a land called Hebron, there lived a very good man named Jacob. He had twelve sons. Of all his sons, Jacob loved Joseph best. Jacob loved Joseph so much that he made him a beautiful coat that seemed to have every color of the rainbow in it. That coat became known as Joseph's "coat of many colors."

Joseph's brothers were jealous that their father loved Joseph more than the rest of them. They were angry at the special way Joseph was treated.

Then Joseph had two dreams that were so remarkable he had to tell his brothers about them. In one dream, his brothers' sheaves of grain were bowing down to Joseph's sheaf. His other dream was about the sun, moon and eleven stars bowing down to Joseph.

His brothers thought Joseph was lying and bragging about the dreams, and they hated him for it. But their father Jacob kept Joseph's dreams in mind.

A short time later, Joseph's brothers were tending sheep far from home. When they saw Joseph coming, his brothers made plans to kill him.

The oldest brother, Reuben, talked his brothers out of their plan to kill Joseph.
 Instead, they took Joseph's coat and threw him into an empty well.

Reuben planned
to come back later
that night and
rescue Joseph from
the well. But before Reuben
could rescue Joseph, a group
of traders came by. Joseph's
other brothers decided that
they would sell Joseph into
slavery rather than kill him.
They sold him for 20 pieces
of silver.

When Reuben came back, he found out what his brothers had done. He was very upset.

The brothers tore Joseph's coat and dipped it in goat's blood. They showed their father Jacob the coat. Jacob was sure that a wild animal had eaten Joseph. He was terribly sad, and none of his family could comfort him.

The traders took Joseph to Egypt where they sold him to Potipher, the captain of Pharaoh's guard. Later, because Joseph was such a good man, Potipher made him the chief servant of his whole house.

Potipher's wife wanted Joseph to love her. But Joseph was loyal to Potipher and he would not obey Potipher's wife. She became very angry.

Potipher's wife made up a lie about Joseph, and Potipher had him thrown into jail. Even there, God took care of Joseph. The keeper of the jail put Joseph in charge of all the other prisoners.

Some years later, while Joseph was still in jail, Pharaoh had two strange dreams. None of his best advisers could figure out the dreams. Finally, a man who had been in prison remembered how Joseph had been able to tell what dreams meant. He told Pharaoh that Joseph could explain his dreams. Pharaoh sent for Joseph.

Joseph said the dream meant that Egypt would have seven years of good crops. Then seven years would pass when nothing would grow and there would be no food. Joseph said that Egypt should store up food from the good years to use when there were no crops.

Pharaoh was amazed at Joseph's wisdom. He made Joseph second in command over all of Egypt. Only Pharaoh himself would be more important than Joseph. Pharaoh gave Joseph fine clothes to wear. He put a gold chain around Joseph's neck and took his own ring and put it on Joseph's finger.

Joseph married an Egyptian girl and they had two sons. The crops increased year by year, just as he had predicted. There were seven good years for all the land.

Then the seven bad years came. The people were hungry and Pharaoh told all the people to go to Joseph and do whatever he said.

Joseph was now the governor of the land. He sold food to all who came. His father Jacob sent all of his brothers except Benjamin to buy food from Egypt. Joseph knew who they were, but Joseph's brothers didn't recognize him after twenty years.

Joseph decided to test his brothers to see if they had changed. Eventually, they proved that they had become much better men. But Joseph still did not tell them he was their brother.

After a while, the brothers came back for more food. This time they brought Benjamin. Joseph finally told them who he was. He told them that it was actually God's will that he was brought to live in Egypt.

Pharaoh heard the whole story and was very happy for Joseph. Pharaoh arranged with Joseph to have his family move to Egypt. They would share in the riches of Pharaoh's kingdom.

All of Joseph's relatives were happy to make the trip to Egypt. Best of all, Joseph's beloved father, Jacob, came with them. Jacob was very glad his son was still alive.

Joseph went out and met his father. They were very happy to see each other. Jacob lived for many more years. He gave his blessing to Joseph's sons. He knew they would be good men, just like their father, Joseph.

Joseph also lived a long and happy life. He knew that God would always take care of his family if they obeyed God's laws.

THE STORY OF MOSES

Long ago, there was a famine in the land of Israel, and the people went to live in the land of Egypt. They found very rich soil in Egypt, and they could grow three or four crops every year. These Hebrew people stayed in Egypt for many years, but they lived apart from the people of Egypt. They worshipped God and stayed away from Egyptian idols.

The Egyptian king, called Pharaoh, saw that there were a lot of Israelites. He was afraid there would soon be more Israelites than there were Egyptians.

He said to his people, "Let us rule these Israelites more strictly. They might turn against us one day."

He made the Israelites work for the Egyptians and build cities for them. But still Pharaoh thought there were too many Israelites. He decided to kill all the baby boys born to the Israelites.

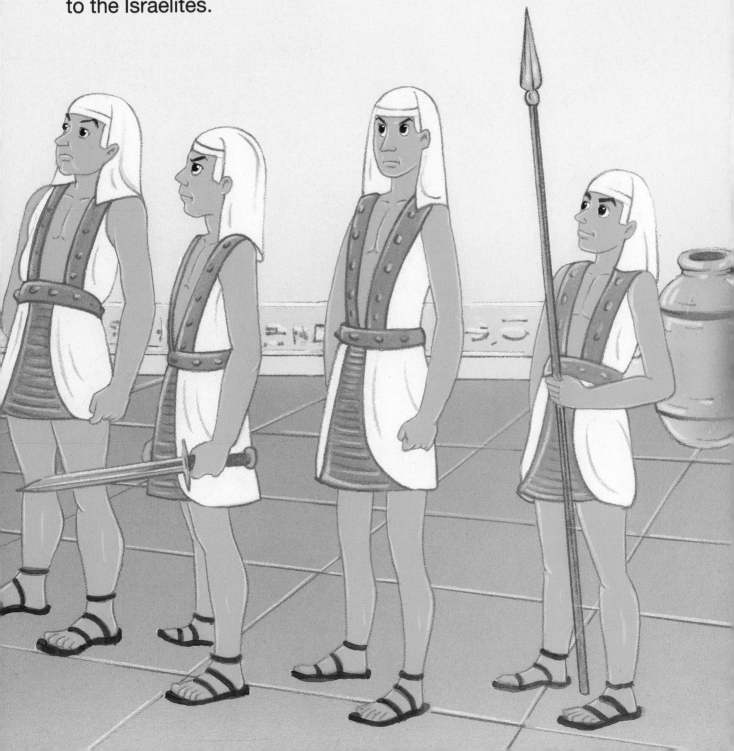

One Hebrew mother wanted to save her baby boy. She put the baby in a small basket and sent his sister Miriam to watch as the basket floated down the river. Pharaoh's daughter saw the basket floating on the water among the reeds when she went to bathe. She opened it and there was a beautiful little Israelite baby. The princess saw Miriam and said to her, "Go find an Israelite woman to take care of the baby."

Miriam went and brought the baby's own mother to the princess. The princess told the mother, "Take this child to your home and nurse him for me, and I will pay you for it."

The baby's mother was happy! No one could hurt her baby son now because he was protected by the princess of Egypt.

When the boy was older, Pharaoh's daughter took him to live in the palace. She named him "Moses," a name that means "to take out," because she had taken him out of the water.

So Moses, the Hebrew boy, lived as the son of the princess in the palace. Even though Moses grew up among the Egyptians, he still loved his own people. The Israelites were poor slaves who served the Lord God.

Moses grew angry with the way the Egyptians mistreated the Israelites. One day he killed an Egyptian. Pharaoh heard about it and Moses ran away. For many years, Moses lived alone in the desert with his flocks. Meanwhile, the people of Israel were working as slaves in Egypt.

One day Moses was watching his father-in-law's animals when he saw a bush on fire. He watched to see the fire burn it up, but the bush kept burning.

Moses heard a voice coming out of the bush, calling him by name. "Moses, Moses! I am the God of your father, the God of Abraham and of Isaac and of Jacob. I have seen how My people suffer in Egypt, and I have heard their cry. I am coming to free them and to bring them up to the Promised Land. You will lead My people out of Egypt. Go and tell them what I have said. Then tell Pharaoh to let My people go."

Moses asked God to give him some sign which he could show the people to prove that God had sent him. God told him to throw his shepherd's staff on the ground.

Moses threw it down. It turned into a snake, and God said, "Take hold of it by the tail."

When Moses did, it again became a staff in his hand.

God said to Moses, "If they will not believe you when you speak My words, show them this sign."

But Moses said, "Oh, Lord, I am not a good speaker."

And God said, "I will teach you what to say."

Aaron, who was Moses' brother, came to meet Moses. God told Moses he would make Aaron the spokesman and Moses would perform the miracles. Together, they went to the people of Israel.

After Moses and Aaron told the Hebrews what God said, they went to see Pharaoh.

"The Lord God of Israel has told us to take our people out of Egypt," they told Pharaoh. "God says, 'Let My people go.'"

Pharaoh was very angry. He said he would not let the Hebrews go. Instead, Pharaoh made the people work even harder.

The Hebrews were upset with Moses and Aaron for making their suffering worse.

Moses and Aaron went back to Pharaoh and again asked him in the Lord's name to let the people go. Pharaoh laughed. "Who is the Lord? Why should I obey His commands? What sign can you show me?"

Aaron threw down his staff, and it turned into a snake. But Pharaoh called his Egyptian wise men and magicians. They threw down their staffs which became snakes, too. But Aaron's staff, in the form of a snake, swallowed them all.

Moses warned Pharaoh that God's punishment, called plagues, would come if he refused to obey God's command. God turned all the water into blood, but Pharaoh *still* would not obey. Then Aaron stretched out his staff and all the land was covered with *frogs*!

Pharaoh said, "Pray to your God for me. Ask Him to take the frogs away, and I will let your people go."

Moses prayed, and God took away the frogs. But after the plague was gone, Pharaoh broke his promise and still held the people as slaves.

God then sent plagues of lice, flies, locusts, deadly animal disease, sickness, hailstorms and darkness. Each time Pharaoh asked Moses to take the plague away. He said he would let the Israelites go, but each time he lied.

God said to Moses, "There will be one more plague, and then Pharaoh will be glad to let the people go. He will drive you out of the land. Get your people ready to leave Egypt."

Moses told his people that at midnight, the Angel of the Lord would go through the land. The oldest child in every house would die unless they found a lamb, killed it, and put the lamb's blood on the frame around the door of each house. They were to roast the lamb and eat it quickly, so they could be ready to march away as soon as the meal was over.

The Israelites did as Moses commanded them. This supper was called "Passover" because when the Angel saw the doors sprinkled with blood, he *passed over* those houses and did not enter them.

As the Angel of the Lord moved through the land, all the people of Egypt became scared. Pharaoh sent a messenger to Moses and Aaron. He said, "Go, get out of Egypt! Take everything that you own. Pray to your God to bless me also."

The Israelites left in a great hurry. To show them the way, God went in front of them in the form of a pillar of clouds during the day and as a pillar of fire at night.

In a few days, the Hebrews came to the shore of the Red Sea. The water was in front of them and high mountains were on each side of them.

Meanwhile, Pharaoh became angry that he had let them go because now he didn't have any slaves. He ordered his army to bring them back.

The Hebrews were upset with Moses. They said, "Why did you bring us out into this terrible place? We are surrounded by the mountains and the sea and our enemies are close behind us. It would be better to be slaves in Egypt than to die here in the wilderness!"

"Do not be afraid," Moses said. "God will save you."
Moses held out his hand over the sea. A mighty east wind
blew over the sea and divided the water. The Hebrews
crossed the sea on a strip of dry land.

When the Egyptians saw the Hebrews marching across dry ground, they followed with their horses and their chariots. But the ground was soft and their chariot wheels got stuck and their horses fell down. The Egyptians became frightened. Moses held out his hand and the sea closed in on them.

God saved all the Hebrews from the Egyptians. Soon they found themselves in a strange land that they had never seen before. This was the land of Sinai where Moses had seen God in the burning bush.

The Israelites traveled for many days through the hot desert until they came to Mount Sinai. God provided everything they needed. They had enough bread, meat and water. Some time later, Moses went up on to the mountain to speak with God.

Moses wanted to find out what God expected him to do next. At last he heard God's voice say, "Moses, if the people of Israel keep My commandments, they will be My chosen people."

God gave Moses the ten laws He wanted His people to keep.

God wrote these commandments on stone tablets with His own finger and gave them to Moses.

I AM THE LORD YOUR GOD; YOU SHALL HAVE NO OTHER GODS BEFORE ME.

YOU SHALL NOT MAKE FOR YOURSELVES A CARVED IMAGE.

YOU SHALL NOT TAKE THE NAME OF THE LORD YOUR GOD IN VAIN.

REMEMBER THE SABBATH DAY TO KEEP IT HOLY.

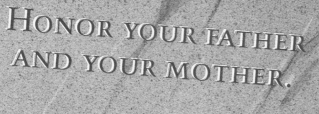

HONOR YOUR FATHER
AND YOUR MOTHER.

YOU SHALL NOT MURDER.

YOU SHALL NOT COMMIT
ADULTERY.

YOU SHALL NOT STEAL.

YOU SHALL NOT BEAR FALSE
WITNESS AGAINST YOUR
NEIGHBOR.

YOU SHALL NOT COVET
ANYTHING THAT IS YOUR
NEIGHBOR'S.

When Moses brought down the tablets, he saw that the people had built an altar to a golden calf. Instead of worshipping God, they were worshipping animals like the Egyptians.

Moses was so angry that he smashed the tablets containing the commandments of God. Then he took the calf and burned it and ground it into powder.

The people of Israel were sorry and accepted God's commandments. God provided Moses with two more tablets to put in a special box called the Ark of the Covenant. Wherever the children of Israel stayed, the Ark was always placed in the middle of the camp.

They took the Ark with them as they marched out across the desert again, and they kept it with them until Moses led them to the Promised Land many years later.

JOSHUA AND THE
BATTLE OF JERICHO

After the time of Moses, the children of Israel were still camped upon the east bank of the river Jordan. God spoke to Joshua, saying, "Now that Moses is gone, you are to take his place. Lead the people across the river Jordan to the land which I have promised to them. Be strong and brave. I will be with you as I was with Moses."

Joshua gave orders to his officers, saying, "Go through the camp and tell the people to prepare food for a journey. In three days we will cross the river Jordan and go into the Promised Land as the Lord has told us."

Then Joshua chose two brave and strong young men. He told them to go as spies across the river and look at the city of Jericho. Before the rest of the land could be claimed, the Israelites would have to capture this city. Joshua told the men to find out all they could about the land.

The two men did as Joshua said and went to Jericho.
But they were spotted by the enemy, and the king of
Jericho sent men to capture them.

The two spies hurried to a house near the wall of the city. The house belonged to a woman named Rahab. She hid the men on the roof of her house and covered them with plant stalks so they could not be seen. The soldiers could not find the spies so they went away thinking that the spies had escaped.

Rahab said, "All of us in this city know that your God is mighty and that He has given you this land. When you capture this city, please promise me that you will spare my life and the lives of my family."

The two men said, "We promise that no harm will come to you, for you have saved our lives."

Rahab let a rope down outside the window of her house so the men could slide down to the ground. They said to Rahab, "When our men come, hang the scarlet cord in the window. We will tell them not to harm the people in the house where they see the scarlet cord."

The two men hid on the mountain for three days. Then they told their story to Joshua.

"It is true the Lord has given us all the land," they said. "The people are afraid of us."

Joshua commanded the people to move their camp. When Joshua gave the word, they marched toward the river Jordan. They stayed there for three days.

Then Joshua said, "Let the priests carry the Ark of the Covenant with the Ten Commandments in front, and let there be a space between it and the rest of the people. Do not come near the Ark."

Joshua said to the priests, "Now walk into the water of the river."

Then a most wonderful thing happened. As soon as the feet of the priests touched the water by the shore, the river

stopped flowing. This left a dry path to go across! The priests carried the Ark down to the middle of the dry river bed.

Joshua gave the order to march across. As the people passed through, the priests stayed in the middle of the river bed, holding the Ark.

Then Joshua called for one man from each of the twelve tribes. He told them to gather twelve stones from the river and build a memorial on the river bed.

When the priests who carried the Ark left the river bed, the river once again began to flow. Now that the children of Israel had reached the land that God had promised to their fathers, they set up a new camp. They built a memorial there just like the one on the river bed.

It was the time of the early harvest, and in the fields they found grain. They gathered it and made bread.

Near the new camp stood the mighty walls of Jericho. When Joshua went out to look at the city, he saw a man holding a sword in front of him. Joshua bravely said to him, "Are you on our side or are you one of our enemies?"

The man said, "Neither. I am the commander of the army of the Lord."

Joshua fell down to the ground and worshipped him. "What does my Lord want me to do?" Joshua asked. The commander of God's army replied, "Take off your sandals. You are standing on holy ground."

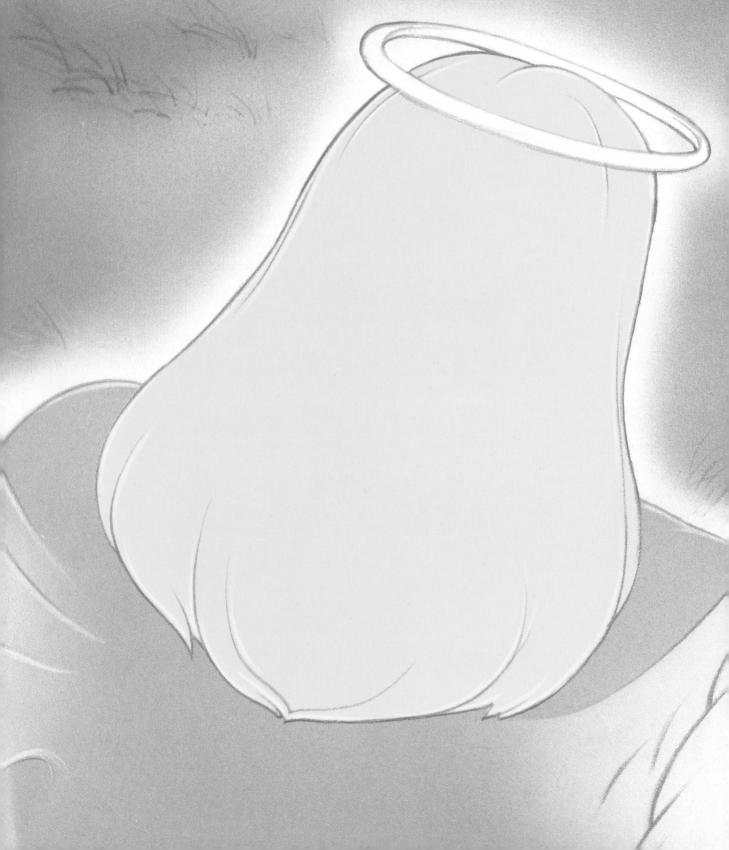

The Lord's commander told Joshua, "I have given the city of Jericho to you."

Then he gave Joshua instructions on how to capture the city.

Joshua went back to the camp and got the people ready to march around the city as God had told him.

In front came the soldiers and next came the priests carrying trumpets made of rams' horns. They blew these long and loud.

Next came the Ark of the Covenant, held on the shoulders of the priests. Last of all came the people of Israel. The only sound was the rams' horn trumpets as they marched around the walls of Jericho. Joshua had commanded the people not to make a sound until he gave the order.

Again the next morning they marched around the walls of the city. They did this each day for six days. On the seventh day, by God's command, they got up very early in the morning. They did not stop when they had marched around the walls once. They kept on marching around and around until they had circled the city seven times.

The seventh time they marched around the city, the priests blew the trumpets. Joshua then said, "Shout! For the Lord has given you the city!"

Then a great shout went up from the people. Everyone looked at the wall and saw it shake and fall with a great crash!

Joshua said to the two brave spies, "Go and bring out Rahab and her family and take them to a safe place."

The two men went into Rahab's house and brought her out with her father and mother and all her family. They cared for them and kept them safely in the camp of the Israelites.

Joshua told the Israelites, "Nothing in this city belongs to you. It is the Lord's and it will be destroyed as an offering to the Lord."

They gathered up all the gold and silver and precious things, and all that was in the houses. They took nothing for themselves, but kept the gold and silver and the things made of brass and iron for the house of the Lord. The rest was burned as Joshua instructed.

Rahab, the woman who had saved the two young spies, was taken in by the people of Israel just as though she had been born an Israelite. One man from the tribe of Judah, whose name was Salmon, took her for his wife. From her children and grandchildren, David was born. David would become the king of Israel.

Rahab was saved and blessed because she had faith in God.

Long ago, there lived a good man named Samuel. He was a prophet and a man of peace and the people loved him. God told Samuel to choose a man named Saul to be King of Israel.

Saul became king and at first he was a good man, but sometimes he didn't do what God told him. This made Samuel angry.

Samuel was sad. He loved King Saul, but he was sad because Saul had disobeyed God's commands. God told Samuel to find someone new to be king.

God told Samuel to go see a man named Jesse. God would choose one of Jesse's sons to be the new king. Jesse had eight sons and he brought seven of them to meet Samuel.

But, one by one, God turned down each one of the seven.

Finally Samuel asked Jesse, "Don't you have another son?" Jesse answered, "Yes, I do—my youngest son David is with our sheep out in the hills."
Samuel told Jesse to get the boy.

God told Samuel that this boy would one day be king of Israel. Samuel gave David a special blessing and then returned home.

David went back to watch over the sheep. They still needed David to protect them with his sling when the lions or bears came around.

David was also a very good musician. When things were peaceful, he liked to play his lyre, which is something like a harp. He played beautiful tunes, making up words to go with them. Many of his words are recorded in the Book of Psalms.

The most famous of David's psalms is Psalm 23, which
is also known as the Shepherd's Psalm:
"The Lord is my Shepherd; I shall not want.
He makes me to lie down in green pastures:
He leads me beside the still waters.
He restores my soul;
He leads me in the paths of righteousness
    for His name's sake.
Yea, though I walk through the valley of the shadow
    of death
I will fear no evil; for You art with me;
Your rod and Your staff, they comfort me.
You prepare a table before me in the
    presence of mine enemies;
You anoint my head with oil; my cup runs over.
Surely goodness and mercy shall follow me
    All the days of my life:
And I will dwell in the house of the Lord
    Forever."

Meanwhile, King Saul was unhappy.
The Spirit of God had left him and he
could not rest.

Saul decided that he wanted someone to come and play music to cheer him up. He asked for David. David's music comforted him and he felt much happier. Whenever Saul was sad David would play for him.

But then there came a war with the Philistines. Saul had to call for an army. David's brothers joined Saul's army but David was still too young. He went back to care for his father's sheep.

The Israelites were afraid because the Philistine army had one very big and very strong soldier. His name was Goliath. He was so tall he looked like a giant.

No man in the army, not even King Saul, dared to go out and fight Goliath. Saul tried to get some of his better soldiers to try, but they were all too scared. Even David's brothers were afraid.

One day, David came to visit his brothers. He was not afraid of Goliath. He was angry at Goliath for insulting God and for scaring everybody.

"If no one else will go, then I will go out and fight this enemy," said David.

The soldiers brought David before King Saul and the King said to David, "You cannot fight this giant. You are too young."

David answered, "I am only a shepherd, but I have fought with lions and bears when they tried to steal my sheep. I am not afraid to fight. The Lord will save me from this enemy, for I will fight for the Lord and His people."

Saul admired David's courage. He told one of his soldiers to put the king's own armor on David. But Saul's armor was much too big for David.

David decided to use his sling, and picked up five smooth stones from a nearby brook. When Goliath saw David, he just laughed. Goliath couldn't believe this boy was going to fight him. But David said, "God will help me."

David chose one smooth stone from his pouch. He took careful aim and slung the stone at Goliath.

The stone struck Goliath square on the forehead with a
loud *thwack*. The giant fell with a *crash*.
David had trusted in the Lord and he won.

When Goliath's army saw him fall, they ran away in fear. King Saul was very proud of David. David was a hero to the King's soldiers and they celebrated his victory over Goliath.

David lived a long life. When he grew up, he became the king of Israel. David is remembered as one of the greatest kings of all time, for he was blessed with the Spirit of the Lord.

Once, long ago, there was a great city. It was called Nineveh and it was so big that it took a person three days to walk all the way around it. It was a large city, and the people who lived there were very mean and wicked.

God wanted someone to warn the people of Nineveh that He was not happy with the way they were living. He decided to send them a prophet. God chose Jonah to tell the people of Nineveh to repent.

Jonah was a very stubborn man. He did not want to preach to the people of Nineveh.

Because Jonah didn't want to do what God had asked, he ran away. He found a ship about to sail to Tarshish, a place far away to the west. He paid the fare and got on board.

Jonah should have known that he could not hide from God. God caused a great wind to blow across the water. Huge waves threatened to sink the ship.

Jonah was sound asleep, but the ship's captain woke him up. He told Jonah to ask God to make the storm stop.

The sailors wanted to know why God was so angry. Why would God bring such a great storm? Jonah told the sailors how he had disobeyed God's orders to go to Nineveh. The sailors were afraid and mad at Jonah for putting them all in danger.

They tried to row the ship, but they couldn't. The sailors asked Jonah what they could do to make the storm stop. Jonah told them to throw him overboard.

They threw Jonah overboard into the sea. The storm stopped, and the water became calm.

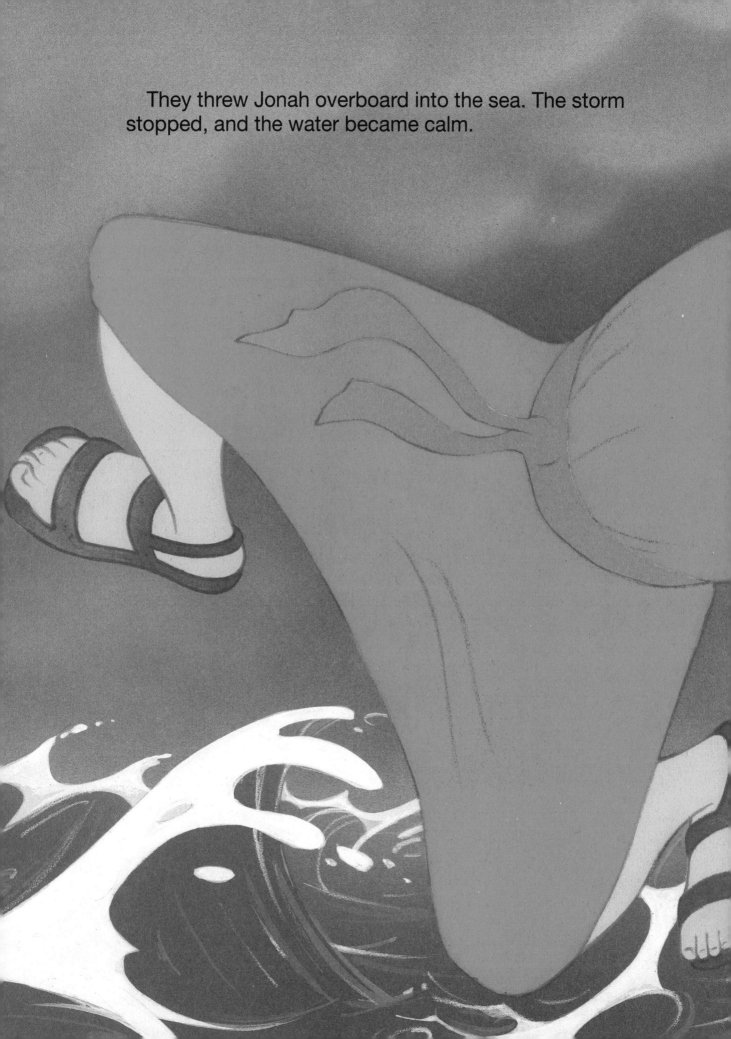

The Lord did not want Jonah to drown. When Jonah was thrown in the water, he was swallowed by a a gigantic fish!

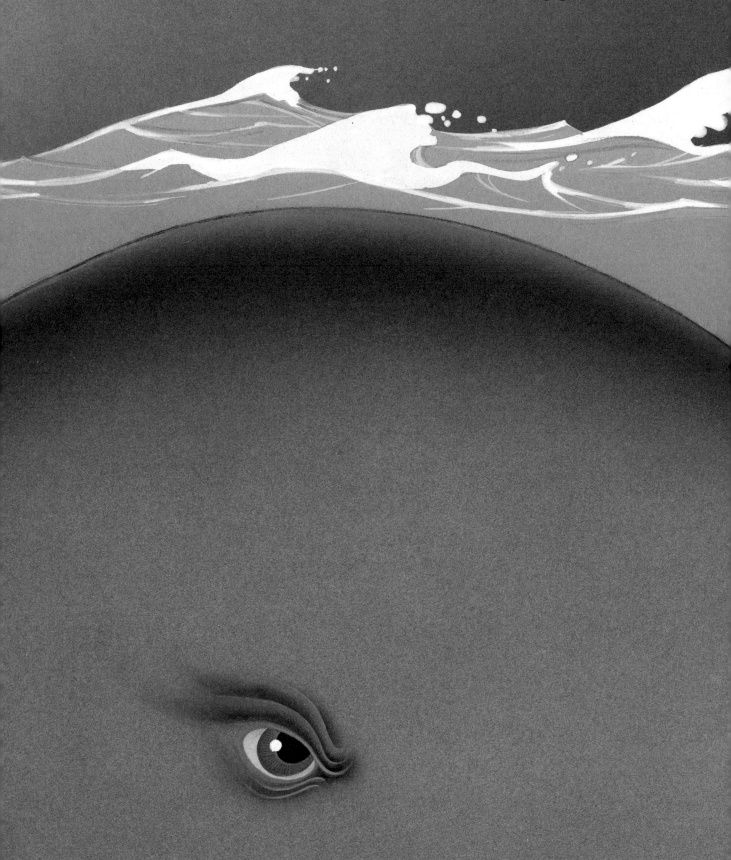

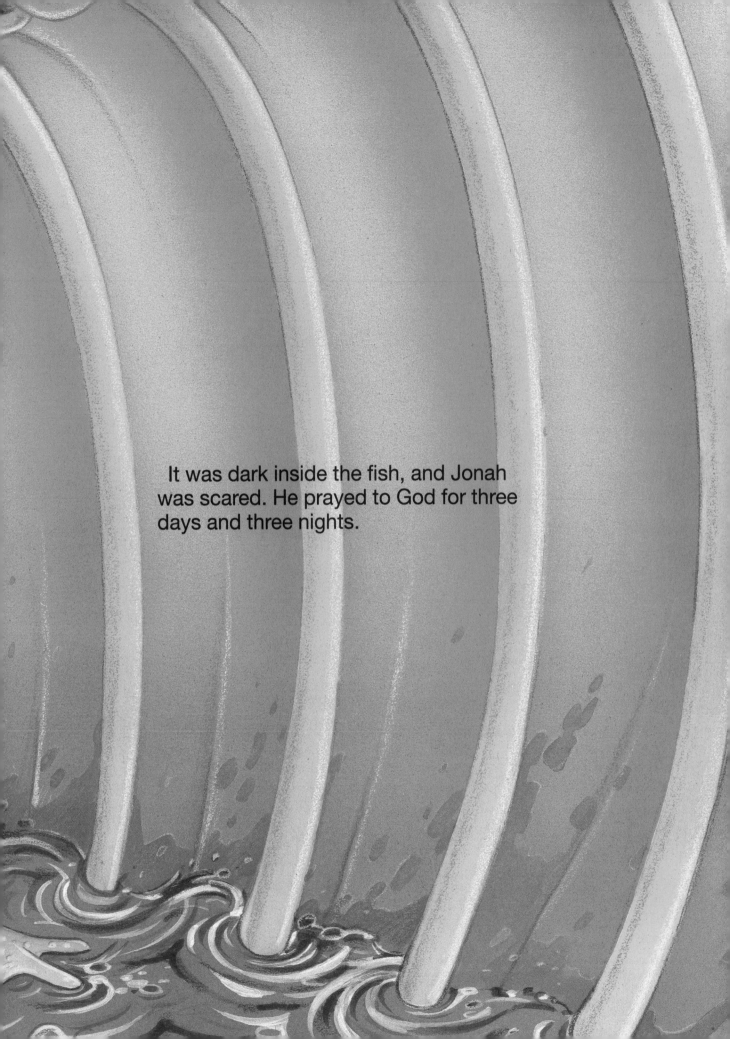

It was dark inside the fish, and Jonah
was scared. He prayed to God for three
days and three nights.

Then God told the fish to spit Jonah out on the coast near Nineveh.

God asked Jonah for the second time to go and warn the people of Nineveh that they must change their ways. This time Jonah obeyed God.

Jonah told the people that they had to live according to God's laws. If they didn't, God was going to destroy their city in forty days.

Jonah was doing what God said, but he wasn't happy.
He didn't like the people in Nineveh. But still he preached,
and the people of Nineveh believed Jonah.

Jonah was surprised. The people of Nineveh changed their ways and prayed to God.

Jonah was mad at God for forgiving the people of Nineveh and not punishing them. Jonah was very angry and miserable.

Jonah was a very stubborn man. He went into the mountains and camped on a spot where he could watch to see if God would change His mind and destroy Nineveh after all. The weather became very, very hot.

Even though Jonah was being stubborn, God felt sorry for him. God made a plant grow up and over where Jonah was sitting. The leaves gave Jonah a lot of shade.

Jonah was thankful for the plant, but that night while Jonah was asleep, God sent a worm to make the plant wither and die. The next day, the sun rose, the wind blew, and it was very, very hot. Jonah was so angry and hot he wished he were dead. But God was teaching Jonah an important lesson.

Jonah had not made the plant grow, but he was mad because it died. God said, "I gave the plant life, like I gave the people in Nineveh life. I care about what happens to them."

Jonah finally began to understand God's message. Jonah saw that he had been very selfish.

Jonah was happy for the first time in a long time. He learned that God loves and takes care of everyone who obeys Him.